TAE KWON DO
B·A·S·I·C·S

Keith D. Yates
6th Degree Black Belt

H. Bryan Robbins
4th Degree Black Belt

 Sterling Publishing Co., Inc. New York

ACKNOWLEDGMENTS

Cover Photos:
Joe Duke

Inside Photography:
Arnold Howard
Joe Duke
C. David Edmonson

Inside Design:
Keith D. Yates

Models:

David Mason
Tony Hyndman
Freddie Pooladsanj
Dallas Ahlmeyer

Jason Gonong
Michael Sherman
Charisse Griffin
Ricky Pickard

10   9   8   7   6   5   4   3

Published by Sterling Publishing Company, Inc.
387 Park Avenue South, New York, N.Y. 10016
Previously published as *Korean Karate*
© 1987 by Keith D. Yates and H. Bryan Robbins
Distributed in Canada by Sterling Publishing
% Canadian Manda Group, P.O. Box 920, Station U
Toronto, Ontario, Canada M8Z 5P9
Distributed in Great Britain and Europe by Cassell PLC
Villiers House, 41/47 Strand, London WC2N 5JE, England
Distributed in Australia by Capricorn Link Ltd.
P.O. Box 665, Lane Cove, NSW 2066
Manufactured in the United States of America

Sterling ISBN 0-8069-8756-1

CONTENTS

Illus. 1.

INTRODUCTION

Learning karate is hard work. It will take you many hours of practice before you can become an expert. You will need to listen closely to what your instructor says and you will need to practise on your own at home. But sometimes it's hard to practise by yourself because you may not know exactly what to do. That's where this book can help. It will show you all the basic exercises and techniques you need to practise in order to develop your karate skills.

You should try to do some of the things in this book every day. You might want to work out with a friend—that way, you can help each other remember all the punches, kicks, and blocks. But be careful when you are practising that you don't hurt yourself or your partner. Remember that karate is a serious art that can be dangerous.

You should only do karate techniques when you are in class or practising at home. Of course, you can also defend yourself with karate, but don't try to show off your moves unless somebody is really trying to hurt you. Good karate students never use their skills unless they absolutely have to.

Where Did Karate Come From?

Karate started many centuries ago in China and slowly travelled from country to country. Today there are many different kinds of karate, with names like *shotokan* and *goju-ryu*. The name for Korean karate is *tae kwon do*. It means "the way of kicking and punching."

What Is a Karate Uniform Like?

The uniform that karate students wear is called a *gi* (ghee) in Japanese and a *do-bok* (dough-bahk) in Korean. It looks like a pair of pajamas, but it's made out of heavy cloth so that it won't tear if somebody grabs it. Most beginners wear an all-white uniform.

The color of the belt indicates your karate rank. All students start out as white belts. You have to take a test to pass to the next-belt rank. The colors sometimes vary from school to school, but they usually are in this order: white, yellow, green, blue, red (or brown), and black.

Illus. 2–4 will show you how to tie your uniform and put on your belt.

Illus. 2. To tie your uniform, cross the right side over first and tie the strings on your jacket. Then, put the left side across and tie those strings. To put on your belt, you need to first hold it up to find the exact middle.

Illus. 2.

Illus. 3. Put the middle part against your stomach. Wrap the belt all the way around your waist and put the left side over the right side. Follow these drawings and be sure to pull your belt tight when you are finished tying it.

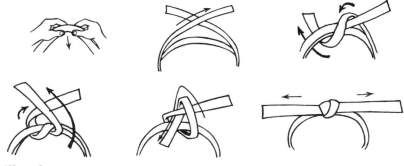

Illus. 3.

Illus. 4. The ends of the belt should be the same length when they hang down.

Illus. 4.

What Is a Karate Class Like?

Every class starts with a bow. We will show you how to bow in this book. A bow is a way of showing respect. That's why you bow to your instructor and to your partner before practice.

Everyone must pay attention in a karate class. You must be quiet, especially during exercises and sparring. Your instructor will tell you when you can ask questions. Never be afraid to ask questions because that is the only way you can make sure you understand.

You should show respect to your instructor in another way besides bowing. Address your instructor formally— such as Mr., Mrs., Miss, or Ms. Smith. Speak to red belts, or brown belts, the same way.

Most karate classes begin with exercises. Then you spend some time learning blocks, punches, and kicks. At the end of class comes sparring practice, when you and a partner get to practise what you have learned. Most schools let students spar only after they have been taking karate for 1 or 2 months.

How Do You Earn a New Rank?

You have to take a test to earn the next-color belt, as we've already said. Usually more than one black-belt instructor gives the test. You have to show them all the things you need to know for the next rank. This includes blocks, punches, and kicks, as well as certain karate forms, self-defense, and sparring. For higher ranks, such as red belt or black belt, you may even have to break some boards. It will probably take you at least 4 years to make black belt.

How Much Do You Need to Practise?

You may go to a karate school that has classes every day. Other students learn from a YMCA or recreation center that has classes only once a week. No matter how many classes you attend, remember that you will learn faster if you also practise at home. When you are getting ready for a test, you should practise every day before the exam for at least 2 or 3 weeks.

Let's Get Started.

We have already said that karate is hard work. You need to pay attention in class and do your best in practice, but it's also important to have fun! Who knows, you might become a black belt in tae kwon do someday!

1
STANCES

Ready Position (*Junbi*)

Illus. 5. Stand with your feet both pointing straight ahead and about one shoulders'-width apart. Hold your fists out in front of your belt.

Illus. 5.

Attention Stance (*Charyo*)

Illus. 6. This stance gets you ready for the bow. Bring your left foot next to your right foot, and place your hands flat against your legs.

The Bow (*Kyungye*)

Illus. 7. Bend forward at the waist, while looking straight ahead.

Illus. 6.

Illus. 7.

Forward Stance (*Chongul Sogi*)

Illus. 8. Start in the ready position.
Illus. 9. Step forward with your left foot. Both feet should be straight ahead and about a shoulders'-width apart (see *Illus. 10*).

Illus. 8.

Illus. 9.

Illus. 10.

Illus. 11. Side view: Bend your front leg, while keeping your back leg straight.

Illus. 11.

Illus. 12. To turn, slide your back foot two shoulder widths straight across behind you.

Illus. 13. Turn around so that you will be facing the other way in a forward balance.

Illus. 12.

Illus. 13.

Back Stance (*Fugul Sogi*)

Illus. 14. Start in the ready position.
Illus. 15. Step forward with your left foot. Your feet should make the shape of the letter "L" (see *Illus. 16*).

Illus. 14.

Illus. 15.

Illus. 16.

Illus. 17. Side view: Bring your hips back over your back leg and then bend both legs.

Illus. 17.

14

Illus. 18. Step forward with your back foot, bringing it next to your front foot. Keep both legs bent.

Illus. 19. Step into a back stance.

Illus. 18.

Illus. 19.

Illus. 20. To turn, pick up your toes on both feet, putting your weight just on your heels.

Illus. 21. Turn your body around in the opposite direction.

Illus. 20.

Illus. 21.

Straddle Stance (Kima Sogi)

Illus. 22. Spread your feet two shoulders' widths apart and bend your knees. This stance is also called a horse or riding stance.

Cat Stance (Goyanghee Sogi)

Illus. 23. This is similar to the back stance, but you place your weight a little farther back and raise your front heel off the floor. It's easier for you to kick with your front leg from this position.

Illus. 22.

Illus. 23.

2
EXERCISES

To be good at karate, you have to be limber. To become limber, you have to stretch your muscles with special exercises. If you do the exercises in this book every day, your body will become more flexible and stronger.

Toe-and-Palm Touch

Illus. 24. Stand with your feet together and your legs straight.

Illus. 25. Bend forward, touching your fingertips to your toes.

Illus. 26. Now touch your palms flat on the floor, keeping your legs straight if you can.

Illus. 25.

Illus. 24.

Illus. 26.

Sitting Stretches

HAMSTRING-MUSCLE STRETCH

Illus. 27. Sit on the floor with your legs spread as far apart as you can get them.

Illus. 27.

Illus. 28. Grab your toes with one hand and pull your head down until you can touch it to your knee. Do this on both sides.

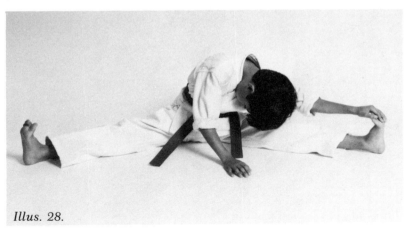

Illus. 28.

Illus. 29. Now try to touch your forehead to the floor in front of you, while keeping your legs straight.

Illus. 29.

GROIN-MUSCLE STRETCH

Illus. 30. Pull your feet together and hold on to them with your hands.

Illus. 30.

Illus. 31. Bend forward, touching your forehead to your toes.

Illus. 31.

Standing Stretches

FRONT-LEG SWING

Illus. 32. Begin in a forward stance.
Illus. 33. Swing your back leg up as high as you can, while keeping it straight.

Illus. 32.

Illus. 33.

SIDE-LEG SWING

Illus. 34. Cross your kicking leg over in front of your other leg.

Illus. 35. Swing your leg up as high as you can. Keep your leg straight and be sure to pull your toes back.

Illus. 34.

Illus. 35.

Partner Stretch

Illus. 36. Sit on the floor with a partner. Put your feet on your partner's knees and grab each other's wrists.

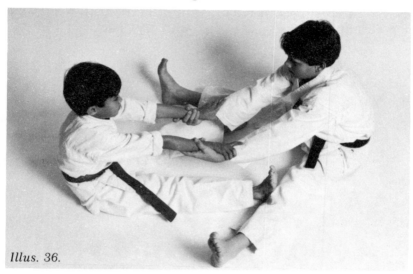

Illus. 36.

Illus. 37. Now lean back and pull. Be careful not to stretch too hard or you might hurt your partner.

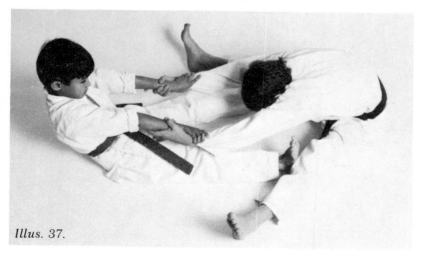

Illus. 37.

Sit-Ups

Illus. 38. Bend your knees and place your hands behind your head.

Illus. 38.

Illus. 39. Sit up without raising your feet off the floor. Place your head all the way between your knees. Practise your sit-ups until you can do 30 without stopping.

Illus. 39.

Push-Ups

Illus. 40. You do a karate push-up on your knuckles. This toughens your hands and makes your wrists strong.

Illus. 40.

Illus. 41. Lower yourself until just your nose touches the floor. Practise until you can do 30 without stopping.

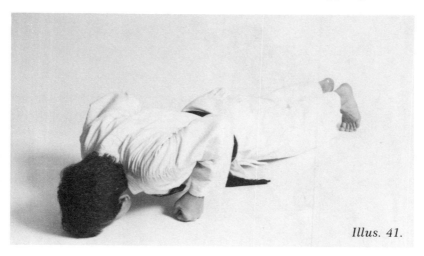

Illus. 41.

Illus. 42. Some instructors allow beginners to do push-ups on their knees and palms until their bodies get stronger.

Illus. 42.

Illus. 43.

3
PUNCHES AND KICKS

How to Make a Fist

Illus. 44. Extend your hand and curl your fingers back. Fold your thumb over your fingers.

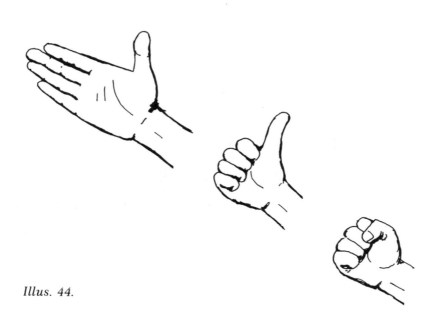

Illus. 44.

Illus. 45. In a karate punch, you strike with your first two knuckles. These knuckles are the largest and will do the most damage.

Illus. 45.

How to Chop

Illus. 46. In the karate chop, or knife-hand, you hit with the side of your hand. You need to keep your fingers together and your thumb folded down.

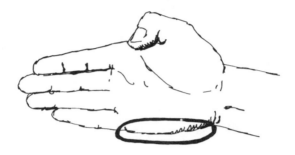

Illus. 46.

Palm-Heel Strike

Illus. 47. This is a good strike for self-defense. Bend your wrist back and fold your fingers in. Strike with the bottom, or heel, of the palm.

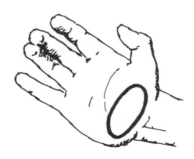

Illus. 47.

Reverse Punch

Illus. 48. Start in a sparring position.

Illus. 48.

Illus. 49. Punch straight out using your first two knuckles. Turn your body as you punch.

Illus. 49.

Ridge Hand

Illus. 50. Start in a back balance.

Illus. 50.

Illus. 51. Strike with the inside ridge of your hand. Make sure your thumb is tucked out of the way.

Illus. 51.

Elbow Strike

Illus. 52 and 53. You can strike with either the front or the back of the elbow. The elbow strike is also good for self-defense.

Illus. 52.

Illus. 53.

Knee Strike

Illus. 54. Bringing your knee straight up between an attacker's legs is very effective, but *be careful not to hurt your partner* when you are just practising.

Illus. 54.

Front Snap Kick

Illus. 55. Start in a forward balance.

Illus. 56. Bring your back foot up to knee level.

Illus. 57. Kick your leg straight out. Pull your toes back so that you won't break them if you hit a hard surface.

Illus. 58. Snap your foot back to your knee. It's as if a rubber band were tied to your leg, quickly pulling it back.

Illus. 55.

Illus. 56.

Illus. 57.

Illus. 58.

Side Snap Kick

Illus. 59. Start in a back balance.
Illus. 60. Bring your front foot up to knee level. Slightly turn your hips to get more power in your kick.
Illus. 61. Kick straight out with the heel of your foot.
Illus. 62. Snap your foot back to your knee.

Illus. 59.

Illus. 60.

Illus. 61.

Illus. 62.

Back Kick

Illus. 63. Look over your shoulder.
Illus. 64. Raise your foot to your knee.
Illus. 65. Kick straight back, striking with your heel.
Illus. 66. Snap your foot back to your knee.

Illus. 63.

Illus. 64.

Illus. 65.

Illus. 66.

Roundhouse Kick

Illus. 67. Start in a back balance.
Illus. 68. Twist your body around, bringing your back leg up in a high fold. Your knee should be higher than your foot.

Illus. 67.

Illus. 68.

Illus. 69. Strike either with the top of your foot (shown here) or the ball of your foot. Your supporting foot should be flat on the ground so that you can keep your balance. *Illus. 70.* Your foot has to come back quickly to keep your opponent from grabbing your leg. Remember to snap it as if a rubber band were tied to your leg.

Illus. 69.

Illus. 70.

Turn Back Kick

Illus. 71. Start in a back balance.
Illus. 72. Look over your shoulder as you raise your foot and start to turn.
Illus. 73. Kick straight back, hitting with your heel.
Illus. 74. Snap your foot back and finish your turn.

Illus. 71.

Illus. 72.

Illus. 73.

Illus. 74.

Hook Kick

Illus. 75. Start in a back balance.
Illus. 76. Raise your front foot, keeping your knee as high as you can.
Illus. 77. Hook your leg out and back, hitting with your heel.

Illus. 75.

Illus. 76.

Illus. 77.

Illus. 78.

4
BLOCKS

Blocks are very important in karate because you have to keep attackers from hitting you before you can hit them back. You need to use your whole body when you block. This means you have to turn your hips a certain way and you have to be in a good stance. The five blocks in this book are the most basic ones. As you get better at karate, your instructor will show you more complicated blocks.

LOW BLOCK

Down Block
(Harden Marki)

Illus. 79. Start in a ready position.
Illus. 80. Fold your left hand over your right shoulder, with your right arm underneath.
Illus. 81. Step forward with your left foot into a forward balance and block down with your left arm. Snap your right fist back to your hip with your palm up.

Illus. 79.

Illus. 80.

Illus. 81.

Illus. 82.

Illus. 82. Fold the hand by your hip on top as before, and twist your upper body as you step through.

Illus. 83. Block down with your top arm.

Illus. 84. To turn, fold the hand by your hip on top as before and twist your upper body as you step through.

Illus. 85. Now turn your body around and block with your top arm.

Illus. 86. **How it works:** You should use the down block for a low attack. Block your opponent's kick with your forearm.

Illus. 83.

Illus. 84.

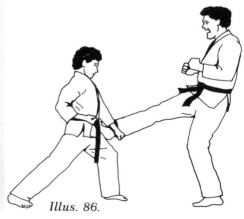

Illus. 85.

Illus. 86.

Up Block
(*Chukyo Marki*)

Illus. 87. Start in a ready position.

Illus. 88. As you step forward with your left foot, raise your right fist over your head and drop your left fist below your belt.

Illus. 89. Finish in a forward balance with your left hand snapping up over your head.

Illus. 87.

Illus. 88.

Illus. 89.

Illus. 90.

Illus. 90. As you step forward with your right foot, reach below your belt with your right hand.

Illus. 91. Finish by bringing your right hand up over your head and your left hand to your hip.

Illus. 92. To turn, bring your left hand down and move your back leg across.

Illus. 93. Now turn your body around and block upwards with your left hand.

Illus. 94. **How it works:** Use the up block for an attack to the top of your head.

Illus. 91.

Illus. 92.

Illus. 93.

Illus. 94.

Inside Block
(Arb Cheegee)

Illus. 95. Start in a ready position.
Illus. 96. Bring both fists up high on your left side with your palms facing out.
Illus. 97. Step forward, snapping your left fist around in front of your face. Bring your right fist to your hip.

Illus. 95.

Illus. 96.

Illus. 97.

Illus. 98.

Illus. 98. Now bring both fists up high to your right side with the palms facing out.

Illus. 99. Step forward with your right leg, snapping your right fist around in front of your face.

Illus. 100. To turn, bring your fists upwards and to the left and move your back leg across.

Illus. 101. Turn your body until your left arm is behind you.

Illus. 102. Block with your arm and bring your right hand to your hip.

Illus. 99.

Illus. 100.

Illus. 101.

Illus. 102.

Illus. 103. **How it works:** You should use the inside block for an attack at your face or chest. Use your forearm to do the block.

Illus. 103.

Outside Block (Yop Marki)

Illus. 104. Start in a ready position.
Illus. 105. Fold your left arm under your right arm, as you step into a back balance.

Illus. 104.

Illus. 105.

Illus. 106. As you finish your step, snap your left arm forward and bring your right hand back to your hip.

Illus. 107. To step forward again, fold your right hand under your left arm.

Illus. 108. Snap your right hand forward and pull your left hand back, as you finish your step.

Illus. 109. To turn, fold your hand on your hip under your right arm.

Illus. 106.

Illus. 107.

Illus. 108.

Illus. 109.

Illus. 110. Snap your left hand out and pull your right hand back.

Illus. 111. **How it works:** You should use the outside block to block a strike to your head or chest. Block with the outside of your forearm.

Illus. 110.

Illus. 111.

Knife-Hand Block (*Sudo Marki*)

Illus. 112. Start in a ready position.

Illus. 113. Open your fists into "knife hands" and raise them over your right shoulder. Your left palm should be next to your right ear and your right hand should be behind your head.

Illus. 114. As you finish stepping forward with your left foot into a back balance, snap your hands around. Your front hand should be facing forward and your back hand should be palm-up in front of your chest.

Illus. 115. Swing your back leg around and bring your hands back to your left side.

Illus. 112.

Illus. 113.

Illus. 114.

Illus. 115.

Illus. 116. As you finish stepping forward, snap your hands around.

Illus. 117. To turn, pivot on your heels and fold your hands up high.

Illus. 118. Snap your hands around, as you finish your turn.

Illus. 119. **How it works:** You should use the knife-hand block to block a strike to your head or chest area. With your hands open, you can grab after you block.

Illus. 116.

Illus. 117.

Illus. 118.

Illus. 119.

5
FORMS

Forms are offensive and defensive movements put together in a pattern that is similar to a dance. They are a very important part of karate training. You must learn new forms each time you want to test for a higher belt rank. The forms in this book are for beginners. As you get better at karate, you will learn more difficult forms.

Your forms should have stable stances and strong blocks, punches, and kicks. As you do them, it's best to pretend you are blocking or striking a real attacker. You should practise forms at home. When you are getting ready to take a test, you should practise them every day.

Heaven and Earth (Chunji)

This is the first form of the International Tae Kwon Do Federation. It is also used by several other Korean karate organizations, such as the World Tae Kwon Do Association and the Southwest Tae Kwon Do Association.

Illus. 120. Start in a ready position.
Illus. 121. Step to the left in a forward balance and do a down block with your left fist.

Illus. 120.

Illus. 121.

Illus. 122. Step forward and punch to the middle.
Illus. 123. Turn all the way around on your right foot and down-block with your right fist.

Illus. 122. *Illus. 123.*

Illus. 124. Step forward and punch.
Illus. 125. Turn to your left and down-block.

Illus. 124. *Illus. 125.*

Illus. 126. Step forward and punch.
Illus. 127. Turn all the way around on your right foot and down-block.
Illus. 128. Step forward and punch. Yell on this step.
Illus. 129. Move your left foot to the left into a back balance. Do an outside block.

Illus. 126.

Illus. 127.

Illus. 128.

Illus. 129.

Illus. 130. Step forward and punch.
Illus. 131. Turn all the way around on your right foot into a back balance and then block.
Illus. 132. Step forward and punch.
Illus. 133. Move your left foot to the left and outside-block.

Illus. 130.

Illus. 131.

Illus. 132.

Illus. 133.

Illus. 134. Step forward and punch.
Illus. 135. Turn all the way around on your right foot and do an outside block.
Illus. 136. Step forward and punch.
Illus. 137. Step forward and punch again.

Illus. 134.

Illus. 135.

Illus. 136.

Illus. 137.

Illus. 138. Step backwards and punch.
Illus. 139. Step backwards and punch again. Yell on this step.
Illus. 140. Move your left foot forward into the ready position.

Illus. 138.

Illus. 139.

Illus. 140.

Providence of the Universe (*Palgue 1*)

This is the first form of the World Tae Kwon Do Federation.

Illus. 141. Begin in a ready stance.
Illus. 142. Turn to the left in a forward balance and down-block with your left fist.

Illus. 141.

Illus. 142.

Illus. 143. Step into a forward balance and outside-block with your right arm.
Illus. 144. Circle your right foot all the way around and down-block.

Illus. 143.

Illus. 144.

Illus. 145. Step forward and do an outside block.
Illus. 146. Move your left foot to the left and down-block with your left fist.

Illus. 145.

Illus. 146.

Illus. 147. Step into a back balance and do a right outside block.
Illus. 148. Step straight forward into a back balance and do an outside block.

Illus. 147.

Illus. 148.

Illus. 149. Step forward into a forward balance and do a right punch. Yell on this step.

Illus. 150. Circle your left foot around into a back balance and do a knife-hand block.

Illus. 149.

Illus. 150.

Illus. 151. Step into a back balance and do a right outside block.

Illus. 152. Circle your right foot around and do a knife-hand block to the right.

Illus. 151.

Illus. 152.

Illus. 153. Step into a back balance and do a left outside block.

Illus. 154. Move your left foot into a forward balance and down-block with your left arm.

Illus. 153.

Illus. 154.

Illus. 155. Opposite view.

Illus. 156. Step forward and do a right reverse knife-hand strike.

Illus. 155.

Illus. 156.

Illus. 157. Opposite view.
Illus. 158. Step forward and do a left reverse knife-hand strike.

Illus. 157.

Illus. 158.

Illus. 159. Opposite view.
Illus. 160. Step forward and do a right punch. Yell on this step.

Illus. 159.

Illus. 160.

Illus. 161. Circle your left foot around into a forward balance and do a left down block.

Illus. 162. Step into a forward balance and do a right outside block.

Illus. 161.

Illus. 162.

Illus. 163. Circle around with your right foot and do a right down block.

Illus. 164. Step forward and do a left outside block.

Illus. 163.

Illus. 164.

Illus. 165. Move your left foot back so that you are in the ready position.

Illus. 165.

Pine Tree Cell
(Song Ahm 1)

This is the first form of the American Tae Kwon Do Association.

Illus. 166. Start in the ready position.
Illus. 167. This is the same position, but seen from the side view. We will demonstrate Song Ahm 1 from this view because it will be easier to see.
Illus. 168. Step forward with your left foot into a forward balance and do a rising block.
Illus. 169. Do a middle punch with your right fist. Do not step forward.
Illus. 170. Do a right front kick.
Illus. 171. Place your foot down in a forward balance and down-block.
Illus. 172. Step forward and punch.

Illus. 166. Illus. 167. Illus. 168. Illus. 169.

Illus. 170. Illus. 171. Illus. 172.

Illus. 173. Shift your right foot back into a straddle stance and outside-block to the right.

Illus. 174. Pull your left foot up to the right and do a right side kick. Yell!

Illus. 175. Place your foot down into a straddle stance and drop your body.

Illus. 176. Step forward with your left foot and punch.

Illus. 173. *Illus. 174.* *Illus. 175.* *Illus. 176.*

Illus. 177. Step forward and do a rising block.
Illus. 178. Punch. Do not step.
Illus. 179. Do a left front kick.
Illus. 180. Place your foot down into a forward balance and do a left low block.

Illus. 177.   *Illus. 178.*   *Illus. 179.*   *Illus. 180.*

Illus. 181. Step forward and punch.
Illus. 182. Shift your left foot back into a straddle stance and do an outside block.
Illus. 183. Bring your right foot to the left and do a left side kick. Yell!

Illus. 181.   *Illus. 182.*   *Illus. 183.*

Illus. 184. Bring your foot down in a straddle stance and chop.
Illus. 185. Step forward and punch.
Illus. 186. Bring your left foot forward into a ready stance.

Illus. 184.   Illus. 185.   Illus. 186.

Freedom (Jayoo)

This is the first form of the Jhoon Rhee system of tae kwon do.

Illus. 187. Begin in a ready position.
Illus. 188. Knife-hand block to the left.
Illus. 189. Do a right punch.
Illus. 190. Pull your left foot to the right and fold your arms.

Illus. 187.   Illus. 188.   Illus. 189.   Illus. 190.

Illus. 191. Knife-hand block with your right arm.
Illus. 192. Do a left punch.
Illus. 193. Pull your right foot to the left and fold your arms.
Illus. 194. Step out and do a knife-hand block.

Illus. 191.   *Illus. 192.*   *Illus. 193.*   *Illus. 194.*

Illus. 195. Do a right punch.
Illus. 196. Step through and fold your arms.
Illus. 197. Knife-hand block with your right arm.
Illus. 198. Do a left punch.

Illus. 195.   *Illus. 196.*   *Illus. 197.*   *Illus. 198.*

Illus. 199. Do a left front kick.
Illus. 200. Step down and do a left punch.
Illus. 201. Do a right punch.
Illus. 202. Swing your right foot around and do a knife-hand block.

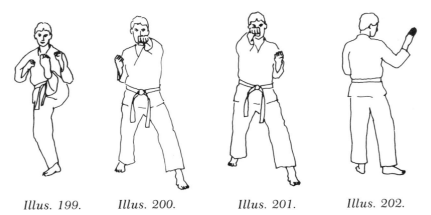

Illus. 199.   *Illus. 200.*   *Illus. 201.*   *Illus. 202.*

Illus. 203. Do a left punch.
Illus. 204. Turn and knife-hand with your left arm.
Illus. 205. Do a right punch.
Illus. 206. Turn to the right and knife-hand with your right arm.

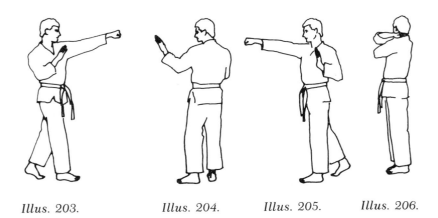

Illus. 203.   *Illus. 204.*   *Illus. 205.*   *Illus. 206.*

Illus. 207. Do a left punch.
Illus. 208. Step and knife-hand with your left arm.
Illus. 209. Do a right punch.
Illus. 210. Do a right front kick.

Illus. 207.   *Illus. 208.*   *Illus. 209.*   *Illus. 210.*

Illus. 211. Step down and do a right punch.
Illus. 212. Do a left punch.
Illus. 213. Swing your left foot around and knife-hand with your left arm.
Illus. 214. Do a right punch.

Illus. 211.   *Illus. 212.*   *Illus. 213.*   *Illus. 214.*

74

Illus. 215. Turn and knife-hand with your right arm.
Illus. 216. Do a left punch.
Illus. 217. Step back to the ready position.

Illus. 215.   *Illus. 216.*   *Illus. 217.*

Illus. 218.

6
ONE-STEPS

One-steps are defensive and offensive movements against an attacker. They are called one-steps because the attacker takes one step forward and punches towards your face. You can either block or move out of the way of the punch, and then strike back with your hands, elbows, knees, or feet.

Karate schools require students to demonstrate various one-steps for belt promotion. Students are graded on their balance, speed, and power. *When demonstrating one-steps at school or practising them at home, you stop just short of hitting your partner in the face.*

Now let's look at four beginning-level one-steps. These photos show the attack with just the right hand, but most instructors want you to demonstrate these moves on both sides (right- and left-hand attacks).

Illus. 218A. The students start in a ready position, facing each other.

Illus. 218A.

Illus. 219. The student on the right does a *kiai* (karate yell) to signal that he is ready. The attacker steps back with his right foot and does a down block with his left arm.

Illus. 219.

Illus. 220. As the attacker steps forward and punches at the defender's face, the defender steps forward with his right foot and does an inside block with his right forearm.

Illus. 220.

Illus. 221. The defender does a back fist with his right hand.

Illus. 221.

Illus. 222. Now he slides forward and punches with his left hand. He yells on the punch.

Illus. 222.

#2

Illus. 223. The student on the left yells to signal that he is ready.

Illus. 223.

Illus. 224. The other student steps back with his right leg and down-blocks with his left arm.

Illus. 224.

Illus. 225. As the attacker steps forward and punches towards the defender's face, the defender slides into a back balance and does an open-hand block with his left hand.

Illus. 225.

Illus. 226. The defender twists his hips and punches with his right hand.

Illus. 226.

Illus. 227. Now he shifts his left hip and shoulder forward and strikes towards the attacker's chin with the heel of his palm. He yells on this strike.

Illus. 227.

#3

Illus. 228. The students start in a ready position. The student on the right yells to show that he is ready.

Illus. 228.

Illus. 229. The attacker steps back with his right foot and does a down block with his left hand.

Illus. 229.

Illus. 230. As the attacker punches towards the defender's face, the defender steps back with his right foot and does an open-hand block with is left hand.

Illus. 230.

Illus. 231. Then he does a front kick with his right leg towards the attacker's stomach or groin.

Illus. 231.

Illus. 232. As he puts his right foot down, he punches with his left hand towards the attacker's face.

Illus. 232.

Illus. 233. Now he twists his hips and punches with his left hand. He yells on the last punch.

Illus. 233.

#4

Illus. 234. The students start in a ready position.

Illus. 234.

Illus. 235. The student on the left yells. Now the attacker steps back with his right leg and blocks down with his left arm.

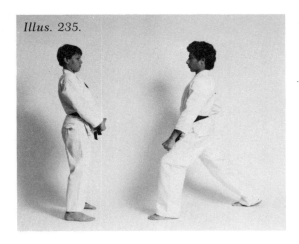

Illus. 235.

Illus. 236. As the attacker punches towards the defender's face, the defender steps to the side with his left leg and does an open-hand block with his left hand.

Illus. 236.

Illus. 237. Now the defender does a round kick with his right leg.

Illus. 237.

Illus. 238. He puts his right foot down in front of his attacker as he punches towards his ribs with his left hand. He yells on the punch.

Illus. 238.

Illus. 239.

7
SELF-DEFENSE

Self-defense is one of the main reasons people take karate lessons. Karate is not just a way to defend yourself against punches and kicks, but also grabs and holds. When you practise self-defense, try to make it as real as possible without hurting your partner. This way, you will be ready for a real fight. Here are some basic self-defense moves. Your instructor will show you many more.

Single Wrist Grab

Illus. 239A. The instructor grabs the student's wrist.

Illus. 239A.

Illus. 240. The student rotates his hand towards the instructor's thumb.
Illus. 241. The student keeps turning his wrist so that he can release the instructor's hold.

Illus. 240.

Illus. 241.

Double Wrist Grab

Illus. 242. The instructor uses both hands to grab the student's wrist.

Illus. 242.

Illus. 243. The student makes a fist with his captured hand. Then he reaches in and grabs his fist with his free hand.
Illus. 244. To escape, he pulls back and up with his entire body.

Illus. 243.

Illus. 244.

Front Choke

#1

Illus. 245. The instructor grabs the defender with a front-choke hold.

Illus. 245.

Illus. 246. The defender brings her arms over his arms and pushes down.

Illus. 247. Then she pushes her right knee towards his groin.

Illus. 246.

Illus. 247.

#2

Illus. 248. The attacker tries to choke the defender.
Illus. 249. She brings her arms over his arms.

Illus. 248.

Illus. 249.

Illus. 250. Now she twists her body to the right and drops her weight down.

Illus. 251. She swings her elbow towards his face. *When you are practising, be careful that you don't strike your partner.*

Illus. 250.

Illus. 251.

#3

Illus. 252. Here is another way to get out of a choke.
Illus. 253. The defender reaches over and under with his left arm.

Illus. 252.

Illus. 253.

Illus. 254. He grasps his own left wrist with his right hand.

Illus. 255. He twists to the left, pushing the attacker's arm up and off his neck with his right elbow.

Illus. 254.

Illus. 255.

#4

Illus. 256. This is another example of an escape from a choke.

Illus. 256.

#5

Illus. 257. The defender swings her hands out and over the attacker's ears. Then she strikes towards his eyes with her fingertips. You should only use this technique if an adult is actually trying to choke you. *When practising this technique, do not really strike your partner's eyes.*

Illus. 257.

Front Bear Hug

Illus. 258. The attacker grabs the defender over both arms.

Illus. 258.

Illus. 259. The defender brings her right leg back.
Illus. 260. Now she drives her right knee towards his groin.

Illus. 259.

Illus. 260.

Rear Bear Hug

Illus. 261. This time the attacker grabs the defender in a bear hug from behind. The defender lifts up his left foot. *Illus. 262.* He drives his heel down hard towards his attacker's foot.

Illus. 261.

Illus. 262.

Illus. 263. He drops his weight down and shoots his arms forward at the same time. This will loosen her hold.
Illus. 264. He drives his left elbow towards her ribs.

Illus. 263.

Illus. 264.

Shoulder Grab

Illus. 265. The attacker grabs the defender by the shoulder.

Illus. 265.

Illus. 266. The defender turns and does an outside block with his left hand.

Illus. 266.

Illus. 267. Now he does a side kick with his left leg towards the attacker's knee. *Be careful when you practise this kick with your partner.*

Illus. 267.

#2

Illus. 268. The attacker grabs the defender's shoulders from behind.

Illus. 269. The defender turns and blocks the attacker's arms off his shoulders.

Illus. 268.

Illus. 269.

Illus. 270. The defender punches with his right fist towards the attacker's ribs.

Illus. 270.

Rear Choke

Illus. 271. This time the attacker is choking the defender from behind.

Illus. 272. The defender steps to the side and brings her arms out in front of her body.

Illus. 271.

Illus. 272.

Illus. 273. She swings a knife hand towards his groin.
Illus. 274. Then she brings her elbow up towards his chin.

Illus. 273.

Illus. 274.

Rear Arm Lock

Illus. 275. The attacker grabs the defender again from behind.

Illus. 276. The defender steps forward and turns to look at the attacker.

Illus. 275.

Illus. 276.

Illus. 277. The defender strikes with a chop towards the side of the attacker's head.

Illus. 278. The defender can finish with a kick towards her kneecap. *This is a dangerous technique, so be careful when you are practising with a friend. Do not make contact when you kick.*

Illus. 277.

Illus. 278.

8
SPARRING

Sparring is an exciting part of karate training. It gives you the chance to test your punches, kicks, and blocks without knowing what your partner is going to do. Some instructors require their students to wear pads on their hands and feet when sparring so that they don't hurt each other.

Many students enjoy tournament sparring. In a tournament, you fight other kids your own age and belt level. You earn points with your kicks and punches. At the end of each match, whoever has the most points wins. If you win enough matches, you may even win a trophy. Whether you win or not, the most important thing is to do your best.

Sparring Stances

Illus. 279. In an **open stance**, both partners face out in the same direction. When sparring you should normally turn your body sideways. This makes it harder for your partner to hit you.

Illus. 279.

Illus. 280. A **closed stance** is when sparring partners face opposite directions. You should learn how to fight in both closed and open positions.

Illus. 280.

Sparring Techniques

Here are some ways to score a point when sparring.

#1 HAND COMBINATION

Illus. 281. The attacker throws a back fist towards the defender's head.

Illus. 281.

Illus. 282. When the defender attempts to block the attacker's back fist, he punches with his back hand. He must be sure to twist his hips. This gives him power and reach.

Illus. 282.

#2 FOOT-AND-HAND COMBINATION

Illus. 283. The partners start in a closed stance. They keep their front hands up to protect their faces and ribs.

Illus. 283.

Illus. 284. The attacker lifts his right leg for a round kick.

Illus. 284.

Illus. 285. He does a round kick towards the defender's groin. The defender should block down with his back hand.

Illus. 285.

Illus. 286. The attacker steps forward with his right leg and punches towards the defender's face with his right hand.

Illus. 286.

ABOUT THE AUTHORS

Sixth-Degree Black Belt Keith D. Yates is president of the Southwest Tae Kwon Do Association and chairman of the board of directors for the Texas Black Belt Commission. He has practised the martial arts for 23 years, and has written 18 magazine articles and three books on the subject. A former state karate champion, he holds additional black belts in the arts of *ju-jitsu* and *kobudo*. Mr. Yates earned a B.A. degree from Southern Methodist University and did his master's thesis at Dallas Theological Seminary on the spiritual aspects of the martial arts. He teaches tae kwon do in Dallas, Texas, where he also works as a graphic design consultant.

Fourth-Degree Black Belt H. Bryan Robbins is assistant professor of physical education at Southern Methodist University. He has studied the martial arts for 16 years. Mr. Robbins was the 1975 and 1976 Pan American Games diving coach and, in 1970 and 1976, was named the coach for the United States Olympic Diving Team. He also holds a second-degree black belt in the art of *aikido,* and has coauthored a book on aikido for beginners. Mr. Robbins has a B.A. from Southern Methodist University and a M.Ed. from the University of Arkansas.

INDEX